Kangaroos

WITHDRAWN

Victoria Blakemore

vblakemore.author@gmail.com

Copyright info/picture credits

Cover, John Crux/Shutterstock; Page 3, Alexas_Fotos/Pixabay; Page 5, Pexels/Pixabay; Page 7, minka2507/Pixabay; Page 9, pjlogan5/Pixabay; Pages 10-11, NoraDoa/AdobeStock; Page 13, worldwildlifewonders/Shutterstock; Page 15, Z Kerth/Shutterstock; Page 17, BellaHomeDecor/Pixabay; Page 19, aly-baba/Shutterstock; Page 21, Sandra Lass/Shutterstock; Page 23; MemoryCatcher/Pixabay; Page 25, Yvinne/Pixabay; Page 27, Squirrel_photos/Pixabay; Page 29, artyangel/Pixabay; Page 31, Broesis/Pixabay; Page 33, John Crux/Shutterstock

Table of Contents

What Are Kangaroos?

Kangaroos are a special kind of mammal called a **marsupial**. This means that the females have a pouch on their stomach.

There are four main kinds of kangaroos. They differ in color, size, and how they live.

Red kangaroos are the largest

kind of kangaroo.

Size

Red kangaroos can be up to five feet long. Their tail can grow to be nearly four feet long. They can weigh up to 200 pounds.

Most kangaroos are smaller than red kangaroos. Many weigh less than 100 pounds.

Male kangaroos, or bucks,

are usually larger than female

kangaroos.

Physical Characteristics

Kangaroos have very strong

back legs. They are used for

hopping and defense from

predators.

Their long tail helps them to

balance when they are

hopping. It is so strong that it

can be used like a leg if they

need to.

They have very good hearing
and, like cats, have ears that
can turn to pick up sounds.

7

Habitat

Kangaroos are able to **adapt** to living in different habitats. They are found in grasslands, deserts, and woodlands.

Most kangaroos live on the ground, but there are some that spend a lot of time in trees.

Kangaroos are found in parts

of Australia and Tasmania.

The red kangaroo is the most **widespread** kangaroo. It is found in most parts of Australia.

Diet

Kangaroos are **herbivores**, which means that they only eat plants.

Most kangaroos spend much of their time **grazing** on grass, while others eat tree leaves, bark, and fruits.

They can go for a long time
without drinking water because
they get much of their water
from plants.

Kangaroos have a special stomach that breaks down the plants they eat. It allows them to eat plant parts that many mammals cannot.

They spend a lot of their time **grazing**. Some spend between seven and fourteen hours each day eating.

Kangaroos use their front

paws to hold their food

when they are eating. 15

Communication

Kangaroos use sound and movement to communicate with each other.

They make sounds such as growls, loud barks, and screaming sounds. Many of their sounds are used as warnings to kangaroos and other animals.

Kangaroos stomp their back
feet as a warning if danger is
near.

Movement

Kangaroos have strong back legs that help them to hop far and fast. Some kangaroos can hop up to thirty feet in a single jump.

Kangaroos have been **observed** moving at speeds of up to thirty-five miles per hour.

Kangaroos have long **tendons** in their back legs. These tendons stretch like springs when they hop.

Kangaroo Life

Kangaroos are very social animals. They live in large groups that are called mobs.

A kangaroo mob can have up to one hundred kangaroos. The kangaroos in a mob touch noses and sniff each other to form bonds.

Most kangaroos are **diurnal**.

They are usually most active

during the day.

Kangaroo Joeys

Kangaroos usually have one baby. Their babies are called joeys.

When joeys are first born, they are about the size of a cherry. They spend the first few months of their life growing in their mother's pouch.

Even when joeys are bigger, they

may still climb into their mother's

pouch if there is danger.

Self Defense

Kangaroos have few

predators, but they are

sometimes hunted by

dingoes.

They can use their strong legs

and sharp claws to protect

themselves if they need to.

They are able to kick, hit, and

scratch.

Kangaroos are more likely to be
hunted by humans than they
are by other animals.

Population

Red kangaroos and gray kangaroos are not currently **endangered**. There are still many left in the wild

The Wondiwoi tree kangaroo is **critically endangered**. There are thought to be fewer than fifty left in the wild.

Kangaroos in the wild usually

live for less than ten years.

Kangaroos in Danger

While not all kangaroos are **endangered**, many are still facing threats. The main threat to most kangaroos is habitat loss.

Many kangaroo habitats are being destroyed for farmland, buildings, and roads.

In some places, people hunt kangaroos. Some are hunted for food and others are for **sport**.

Helping Kangaroos

Special **preserves** protect animals like kangaroos. They provide these animals with a safe place to live.

In some places, signs are along roads where kangaroos live. They warn people to watch for kangaroos when they are driving.

Some zoos have special programs to help kangaroos. They train young kangaroos to survive in the wild. When they are ready, they can be released into the wild.

The goal of all of these programs is to help kangaroos. People want to prevent them from becoming **extinct**.

Glossary

Adapt: to change or adjust

Critically Endangered: when an animal is nearly extinct

Diurnal: most active during the day

Endangered: at risk of becoming extinct

Extinct: when there are no more of an animal left in the wild

Grazing: eating grass

Herbivore: an animal that eats only plants

Marsupial: an animal that has a pouch on its stomach where the babies are kept until they are old enough to feed themselves

Observed: noticed or seen

Preserves: areas of land set up to protect plants and animals

Sport: something done for fun

Tendons: a cord of tissue that connects muscles and bones

Widespread: found in a wide area

About the Author

Victoria Blakemore is a first grade

teacher in Southwest Florida with a

passion for reading.

You can visit her at

www.elementaryexplorers.com

Also in This Series

Also in This Series